Potbellied Pigs

Pamela Tasker

PowerKiDS press.

New York

Published in 2018 by The Rosen Publishing Group, Inc.
29 East 21st Street, New York, NY 10010

First Edition

Editor: Melissa Raé Shofner
Book Design: Mickey Harmon
Interior Layout: Rachel Rising

Photo Credits: Cover optimarc/Shutterstock.com; Cover, p. 1 AngelaLouwe/Shutterstock.com; p. 5 Mother Daughter Press/ Photographer's Choice/Getty Images; p. 6 GK Hart/Vikki Hart/Photodisc/Getty Images; p. 7 Aumsama/Shutterstock.com; p. 8 Eric Isselee/Shutterstock.com; pp. 9, 11 Galyna Andrushko/Shutterstock.com; p. 13 Yatra/Shutterstock.com; p. 14 Tischenko Irina/Shutterstock.com; p. 15 Westend61/Getty Images; p. 17 Dave Blackey/All Canada Photos/Getty Images; p. 18 Abel Tumik/Shutterstock.com; p. 19 Bill Greenblatt/Hulton Archive/Getty Images; pp. 20, 22 © iStockphoto.com/chengyuzheng; p. 21 MintImages/Shutterstock.com.

Cataloging-In-Publication Data
Names: Tasker, Pamela.
Title: Potbellied pigs / Pamela Tasker.
Description: New York : PowerKids Press, 2018. | Series: Our weird pets | Includes index.
Identifiers: ISBN 9781508154204 (pbk.) | ISBN 9781508154143 (library bound) | ISBN 9781508154020 (6 pack)
Subjects: LCSH: Potbellied pigs as pets—Juvenile literature.
Classification: LCC SF393.P74 T37 2018 | DDC 636.4'0887—dc23

Manufactured in the United States of America

CPSIA Compliance Information: Batch #BS17PK: For Further Information contact Rosen Publishing, New York, New York at 1-800-237-9932

Contents

A Pig for a Pet!

You may have seen pigs on a farm, rolling around in the mud. Many people wouldn't think of bringing a pig into their home as a pet. However, potbellied pigs make wonderful pets!

Potbellied pigs are smart and surprisingly clean animals. They're playful and curious and can even be trained! When properly cared for, they can be loving companions for many years. Read on to find out if a potbellied pig might be the pet for you.

PET FOOD FOR THOUGHT

Potbellied pigs usually live for 12 to 18 years, but some may live longer. Will you be able to care for a pet this long?

Potbellied pigs need lots of food and space to play. They make great pets, but they aren't right for everyone.

5

Big Little Pigs

Most potbellied pigs grow to be about 125 pounds (56.7 kg). However, some may weigh more than 200 pounds (90.7 kg)! Even though these pigs weigh a lot, they aren't very big. Most are around 2 feet (0.6 m) tall, though some may be a little shorter or taller.

Potbellied pigs are solid, meaning they're heavy but their bodies are small. Potbellied pigs often weigh more than dogs that are larger than them.

PET FOOD FOR THOUGHT

Potbellied pigs have poor eyesight, but they can smell and hear very well.

Potbellied pigs can be all black, or white with black spots. Pigs with white hair often look pink because of their skin color.

The potbellied pigs that are kept as pets are originally from Vietnam. They're considered a type of **miniature** pig. Potbellied pigs may not seem so small. However, they're quite small compared to farm hogs, which can weigh more than 1,000 pounds (453.6 kg)!

Potbellied pigs were first brought to the United States in the mid-1980s. They weren't meant to be pets, but people soon realized they made great companions.

farm hog

PET
FOOD
FOR
THOUGHT

The first potbellied pigs sold as pets in the United States were larger than those sold today. They originally cost several thousand dollars, but today they cost much less.

In the wild, Vietnamese potbellied pigs sometimes form large herds. Herd members use many sounds to communicate, or talk, to each other. They may squeak, grunt, or even sneeze!

Picking a Pig

Before bringing home a potbellied pig, you should spend time learning about their needs and the costs of owning one as a pet. If you and your family have enough time, money, and space to care for a pig, you should first check a local **animal shelter** for pigs that are up for adoption.

You may also find potbellied pigs for sale by a trusted **breeder**. Remember that potbellied pigs will grow to be quite heavy. Someone selling pigs that will "stay small forever" shouldn't be believed.

PET FOOD FOR THOUGHT

Check your local laws to be sure potbellied pigs are allowed where you live. It's against the law to own them as pets in some places because they're considered livestock.

Potbellied pigs aren't fully grown until they're about three years old or older. They get their name from the round shape of their belly.

A Place for Your Pig

Potbellied pigs can live in your home. Be sure to give your pig a place of its own where it can feel safe. This might be a quiet room, a special sleeping box, or a cage. Give your pet some old blankets and pillows to sleep on.

If you prefer to keep your potbellied pig outside, make sure it has a windproof and rainproof house to live in so it stays warm and dry. Potbellied pigs also need lots of shade because they can get a sunburn just like people can.

PET FOOD FOR THOUGHT

Never leave your potbellied pig alone with a dog. Pigs have no way of guarding themselves from a dog attack. Make sure dogs and other animals can't get into your pig's outdoor pen.

Indoor pigs need time to play outside in a fenced-in area. This will help keep them happy and healthy.

Pig Out!

Potbellied pigs love to eat and may easily become overweight. To keep your pig healthy, talk to your vet about the proper amount of food to feed your pet. Younger pigs and active pigs need more food than those that are older or less active.

You can find potbellied pig food online or at a pet store. These foods are specially made for potbellied pigs. They contain the perfect balance of **nutrients** to keep your pet healthy. Always make sure your pig has fresh water to drink.

PET FOOD FOR THOUGHT

Some people think potbellied pigs will stay small if they aren't fed a lot, but this is wrong and unsafe. Underfeeding your pet can make it very sick.

You can feed your potbellied pig fresh vegetables, too. Just don't feed it too many. Vegetables should only be 25 percent of what your pet eats each day.

15

Clean Piggies

Potbellied pigs are clean animals that don't need regular bathing. If your pig does get dirty, it's fine to hose it off. However, potbellied pigs have naturally dry skin and bathing them too often can make it worse. You can rub a little **lotion** onto your pet's skin if it gets overly dry.

Potbellied pigs have **coarse** hair on their body that they shed, or lose, once or twice a year. This will make your pet **itchy**. Brush your pig to help remove loose hair.

PET FOOD FOR THOUGHT

Pigs only sweat through the top of their nose, so they overheat easily. Make sure your pig has lots of shade when it's outside. You can also give your pet a small pool of water to keep cool in.

Potbellied pigs learn to go to the bathroom in a certain spot. Your pet can be trained to use a **litter** box or go outside to do its business.

17

Visiting the Vet

Before you bring home a potbellied pig, make sure there's a vet in your area who knows how to properly treat your new pet. Many vets don't deal with pigs often, if ever. Potbellied pigs are not treated the same as farm pigs.

Take your pig to the vet for a checkup every year. Your pet needs special shots so it doesn't get worms or certain illnesses. If your pig is acting strange or doesn't want to eat, it may be sick.

multivitamin

PET FOOD FOR THOUGHT

You may give your potbellied pig one children's **multivitamin** each day to help keep it healthy.

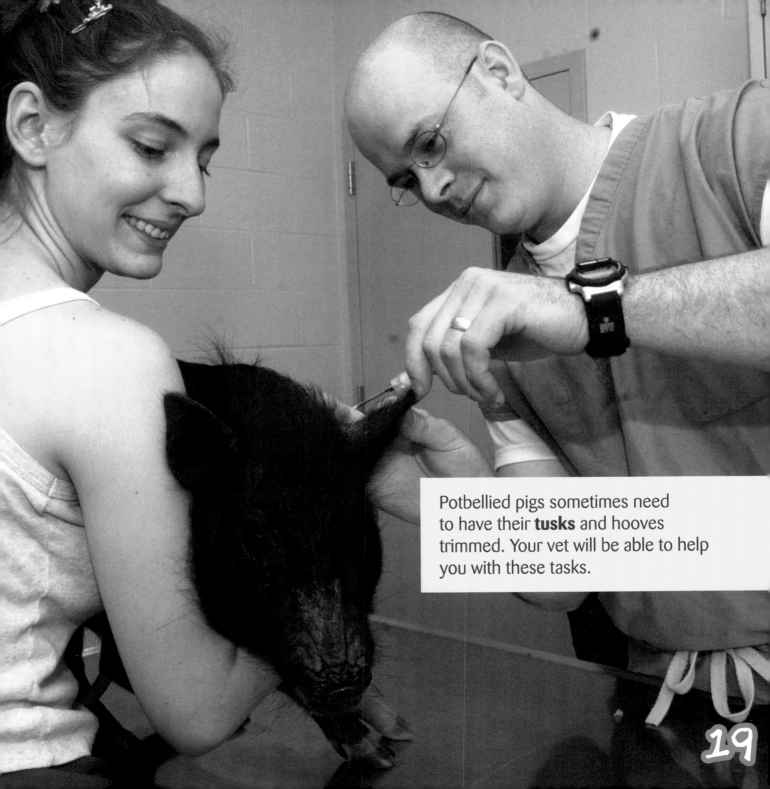

Potbellied pigs sometimes need to have their **tusks** and hooves trimmed. Your vet will be able to help you with these tasks.

19

Playful Pigs

Potbellied pigs enjoy being close to their owners and love to play with toys. Pigs like to root, or dig up earth with their snout. Keep your pet busy by filling a box with large rocks for them to root around in. You can sprinkle in treats they can hunt for.

Potbellied pigs can be trained to do tricks. You can use popcorn or cereal to train your pig. If you buy a **harness** for your pig, you can take it for walks!

PET FOOD FOR THOUGHT

Don't try to pick up your pet pig. Potbellied pigs can be heavy, and they don't like to be hugged or held. It may scare them and make them uncomfortable.

Potbellied pigs may figure out how to open cupboards or the refrigerator. Special baby locks and gates will keep your pet out of places it shouldn't go.

21

Potbellied Pig Care Fact Sheet

- Your potbellied pig needs a safe space to call its own.

- Give your pig blankets to sleep on.

- Keep your potbellied pig out of direct sunlight.

- Don't overfeed your potbellied pig!

- Make sure your pet always has fresh drinking water.

- Feed your pet special potbellied pig food and a small amount of vegetables.

- Find a vet who knows how to care for potbellied pigs.

- Take your pet for yearly vet checkups.

Glossary

animal shelter: A place where people take lost animals or animals without an owner.

breeder: A person who brings male and female animals together so they will have babies.

coarse: Thick and rough.

harness: A set of straps that goes around an animal's body, often used to control it.

itchy: Having an uneasy feeling on the surface of the skin.

litter: Material used to absorb the waste of animals.

lotion: A liquid that is put on the skin.

miniature: Something that is small for its kind.

multivitamin: A pill containing several nutrients to help the body fight illness and grow strong.

nutrient: Something taken in by a plant or animal that helps it grow and stay healthy.

tusk: A long, large pointed tooth that comes out of the mouth of some animals.

Index

Websites

Due to the changing nature of Internet links, PowerKids Press has developed an online list of websites related to the subject of this book. This site is updated regularly. Please use this link to access the list: www.powerkidslinks.com/owp/pbpig

24